Fragrance and Flower Craft

Fragrance and Flower Craft

Joanna Sheen

a Salamander book

Published by Salamander Books Limited
LONDON

Published by Salamander Books Limited
129-137 York Way
London N7 9LG
United Kingdom

1 3 5 7 9 8 6 4 2

ISBN 0-517-14025-X

Distributed by Random House Value Publishing, Inc.
40 Engelhard Avenue
Avenel, New Jersey 07001

A CIP catalog record for this book is available
from the Library of Congress

CREDITS

Editor: Jane Struthers
Design: Roger Daniels
Cover design: Colin Robson
Photographers: Jon Stewart and Sue Atkinson
Typesetting: Pearl Graphics
Color reproduction: Regent Publishing Services and Classic Scan
Printed in Italy

ACKNOWLEDGEMENTS

The publishers would like to thank the following for supplying
materials used in this book:

G Baldwin and Co, 173 Walworth Road, London SE17 1RW
(pot pourri ingredients)
Culpepper Limited, 21 Bruton Street, London W1X 7DA
(pot pourri and cosmetic ingredients)
The Diddybox, 132-134 Belmont Road, Astley Bridge, Bolton, Lancashire BL1 7AN
(general flower arranging equipment, silica crystals and some pot pourri ingredients)
Joanna Sheen Limited, PO Box 52, Newton Abbot, Devon TQ12 4YF
(pressed flower equipment, dried flowers, pot pourri ingredients and other craft items)
Teign Valley Glass, Pottery Road, Bovey Tracey, Devon TQ13 4YF
(hand-blown glass and scent bottles)

CONTENTS

INTRODUCTION

Flowers can be a constant source of pleasure, and a bonus when you dry or press flowers is their extended life. One of the most important ingredients of any natural thing is its smell – flowers and mosses, trees and grass, everything has its own special fragrance. The perfume contained in flowers varies from simple scents, such as those of honeysuckle and jasmine, to the headier aromas of old roses and hyacinths. Everyone has their favourites – bluebells in the spring or autumn leaves and moss, all have a particular place in the palette of flower fragrances that you can collect and blend together. A glossary of essential oils is featured at the back of the book, which will help you to choose scents for exotic creams and perfumes and heady pot pourris of your own.

In this book there are many beautiful gift ideas that will delight friends and relatives or you can even make them for yourself. All the projects shown in the following chapters are simple to make, providing you follow the instructions carefully. They will bring hours of pleasure to the recipient, and you will have a lot of fun making them as well. The raw materials can either be bought, or harvested from your own garden or that of a friend. Alternatively, keep your eyes open when walking in the countryside, where there are often fallen cones or nuts you can use in your craft work. Silk flowers are always interesting to work with, they don't fade or droop and a wonderful selection is available from department stores and small craft shops or florists. Although they are fairly expensive, it only takes a few blooms to make something really eye-catching, so they can be a worthwhile investment.

Also included are some ideas for using flowers in the kitchen. Edible flowers are slowly gaining in popularity, although they are an acquired taste! However, the selection of teas, vinegars, honey and mustard would all be very acceptable as a gift or on the family breakfast or dinner table. Hopefully the dozens of ideas contained in the book will inspire you to think of many more and to use your own artistic ability to create even more original and wonderful crafts.

DRYING HERBS AND FLOWERS

Many of the projects in this book use preserved flowers that have been pressed, dried or preserved in silica gel crystals, and the techniques are explained fully on these pages. The method you choose will depend partly on personal preference and also on which particular project you are making.

PRESSED FLOWERS

Garden and wild flowers can all be pressed with a minimum amount of equipment and by following a few simple instructions. Choose fairly flat flowers, not thick-centred, multi-petalled blooms. Pick the flowers when they are completely dry – about mid-morning on a dry day. Only harvest really fresh, new flowers – if you put rubbish into a press you will get rubbish out.

A flower press can be bought from a craft shop or department store and consists of 2 pieces of wood with holes drilled in each corner. A set of 4 bolts are inserted through the holes and a screw fitting placed on the end of each bolt. The contents of the press should be 20 pieces of good quality blotting paper interspersed with thick pads of newspaper. If you buy a press and there are pieces of card inside, throw them away and replace with sheets of newspaper.

Having picked some fresh, dry material, you need to place it in the press. Open the press and place some newspaper on the bottom, then put a sheet of blotting paper on top. The flowers should have any stalks or pieces that stick out unneccessarily trimmed off, then the flowers can be placed on the blotting paper, with space between each flower or leaf. Cover this layer with another sheet of blotting paper and then some more newspaper. Continue to build up the layers in the press until you have used all the papers. Screw down the press tightly and label with the date and contents. The press should then be put in a warm dry place and left for about 6 weeks. After that time the flowers will be ready to use and can be removed from the press.

DRYING IN THE MICROWAVE

Many households have a microwave oven now and this can be a very quick and useful way to dry small quantities of herbs and flowers for culinary purposes or for making cosmetics or pot pourri. Drying plant material quickly in the microwave does not enhance its shape and, therefore, is not recommended when you want the material for decorative use.

Lay a sheet of absorbent kitchen paper in the bottom of the microwave oven and place a small bunch of herbs or flowers on the paper. Experiment with different settings and timings, but to start with try a medium setting for 2 minutes. The plant material must be completely dry; if it is not then leave it in the microwave for a little while longer. Microwave ovens vary from model to model, so it is difficult to give exact timings – a little experimentation on your part will soon tell you how long you need in your particular oven. Keep checking the herbs or flowers to see if they are dry, as they can swiftly turn from thoroughly dried plant material to a pile of desiccated cinders!

AIR DRYING

The oldest and simplest way of preserving plants is to make small bunches and fasten them with an elastic band. It is important to use an elastic band rather than string, otherwise when the stems dry out and shrink, the bunch will disintegrate and end up on the floor. Gather a small bunch, secure with an elastic band approximately 2.5-5 cm (1-2 in) down the stems and hang in a dry, airy position. Many people dry bunches of herbs in their kitchen – the suitability of your kitchen will depend upon how much light and steam affects the area where you intend to dry things. Above an Aga or kitchen range can be a very successful place for drying, provided the plants are kept out of the way of the steam from pans on the top of the cooker. Alternatively, any dry, warm corner of the house will suffice.

It will take from a few days to several weeks to dry the flowers or herbs, depending upon the variety and where they have been hung to dry. Once you are sure they are completely dry, wrap them loosely in tissue paper and store in a suitable box. A long flower box from the florist is ideal if you first cover the holes that serve as handles each end, so that your precious stores are not invaded by insects or mice. It is important to keep your dried flowers or herbs in a reasonably warm, constant atmosphere. A garage is fine in a warm climate or a hot summer but should be used as a very last resort at any other time of year because it is likely to be too damp.

DRYING IN SILICA GEL CRYSTALS

To obtain perfect results when drying individual flowers, silica gel crystals are the answer. These crystals remove the moisture from the plant materials but keep the colour and shape perfectly, making them particularly useful for decorating the top of a mix of pot pourri. The crystals may be available from your local florist or garden centre; if not, try one of the mail order sources listed at the front of the book. The crystals are expensive but can be used many, many times.

The crystals often come in a plastic container, and this can be used for the drying process. Empty the crystals into a bowl and then spoon some back into the bottom of the plastic container to a depth of about 2.5 cm (1 in). Stand flower heads in the 2.5 cm (1 in) of crystals and, with a teaspoon, carefully cover them with more crystals, filling every crevice and gap until they are completely buried. Place the lid on the box and leave them for about a week, then carefully unpack them with a teaspoon, taking care not to damage the very brittle flowers. The dried flowers should be stored in an airight container with a few crystals to keep them free from damp. To discourage any reabsorption of moisture, you can spray the flowers with some light polyurethane varnish. You can only dry the flower heads so a false stem will have to be wired on should you wish to use the flower in an arrangement.

DRYING PETALS AND SMALL ITEMS

To dry individual petals or small items like cones, spread them out on a wire rack used for cooling cakes and leave them in a warm room or, better still, a warm airing cupboard, until they are completely dry. They should then be stored in an airtight container in a dry atmosphere.

POT POURRI INGREDIENTS

Pot pourri can include almost anything you choose, as you will see from the recipes that follow. If you want to dry leaves or flowers very rapidly for use in pot pourri, they can be dried in a conventional oven or in a microwave (see above). Their shape will distort and often the colour alters but this does not matter when they are destined for a pot pourri mix. It is still wise to choose prime materials for drying but you can also use petals or flower heads that have dropped off your arrangements or fallen while they have been hanging up to dry. The ingredients that are harder to find, such as orris root or unusual spices, can be obtained by mail order from several firms and these are listed at the front of the book. Likewise, the oils are usually available from many high street outlets (check before buying that they are essential oils and not blends of oils) but if you have difficulty locating the exact fragrance that you want, then there are mail order sources that may be able to help.

GROWING INGREDIENTS IN YOUR GARDEN

Many of the ingredients used in this book can be grown in small gardens or even in window boxes. Growing herbs can be a very rewarding pastime, as you can enjoy the plants in the garden and also your cookery and other hobbies, such as making your own cosmetics, will be much more interesting. Alternatively, larger supermarkets now sell fresh herbs, which you can dry, and it is worth looking around local health food stores as they may have many of the ingredients that are needed.

POT POURRI

Place 250 ml (9 fl oz/1 cup) lavender flowers in a bowl and add 115 ml (4 fl oz/½ cup) each of the following: dried mint, marjoram and oregano flowers. Add 250 ml (9 fl oz/1 cup) small green leaves to this mixture.

Mix all these ingredients well and then add 30 ml (2 tbsp) orris root powder.

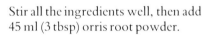

Finally, add 10 ml (2 tsp) lavender oil, using either essential oil or a pot pourri oil. Mix well with a metal spoon. Place the mixture in a plastic bag and leave to mature for about 2 weeks, shaking regularly. Once matured, display the pot pourri in a suitable container.

In a large bowl, mix together 450 ml (16 fl oz/2 cups) dried red rose petals, 250 ml (9 fl oz/1 cup) lavender and 115 ml (4 fl oz/½ cup) dried marjoram. Add 15 ml (1 tbsp) cloves, 115 ml (4 fl oz/½ cup) dried orange peel and 6 nutmegs. Break 3-4 cinnamon sticks into the mixture as well.

Stir all the ingredients well, then add 45 ml (3 tbsp) orris root powder.

Add 15 ml (1 tbsp) of any rose pot pourri oil and stir well – use a metal spoon rather than a wooden one as wood absorbs the oil. When the oil is well mixed in, place the mixture in a plastic bag and seal. Leave to mature for 2 weeks, shaking occasionally, and then turn into a bowl to display.

In a large bowl, mix together 250 ml (9 fl oz/1 cup) dried orange peel and 30 ml (2 tbsp) orris root powder.

Add 15 ml (1 tbsp) sweet orange essential oil and 15 ml (1 tbsp) mixed spice essential oil to this basic mixture.

Mix in 685 ml (24 fl oz/3 cups) assorted cones, acorns etc and stir well. Place all the ingredients in a plastic bag and seal. Leave the mixture for at least 2 weeks, shaking the bag regularly, then display in a pretty basket.

The dried apple slices for this pot pourri can be dried in the bottom of the oven on a low temperature for several hours. In a bowl, mix together 250 ml (9 fl oz/ 1 cup) of each of the following: peach stones, rosehips, beech masts, larch cones and star anise. Add 3 or 4 whole or cracked nutmegs and 6 broken cinnamon sticks.

Add to this mixture 60 ml (4 tbsp) orris root powder and mix in well. Add 15 ml (1 tbsp) allspice essential oil and 15 ml (1 tbsp) sweet orange essential oil and mix thoroughly with a metal spoon.

Add 250 ml (9 fl oz/1 cup) dried apple slices. Place the mixture in a plastic bag and leave to mature for about 2 weeks, shaking regularly. Once matured, display the pot pourri in a suitable container.

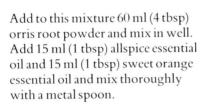

The shells can be collected from the beach, or you can buy shells from many craft shops. You will need the following ingredients: 1 cup assorted shells, a handful oak moss, 6 cinnamon sticks, 1 cup dried blue larkspur flowers, nigella seed heads and beech masts, 30 ml (2 tbsp) orris root powder and 20–30 drops of any essential oil of your choice.

Place all the ingredients, except the orris root powder and oil, in a mixing bowl and mix well together. Add the orris root powder and mix in well. Finally, add 20–30 drops of the oil of your choice and mix in well with a metal spoon until it is completely absorbed.

This subtle and aromatic pot pourri is especially suitable for a kitchen or dining room. You will need a handful of each of the following dried ingredients: scented geranium leaves, marjoram and oregano flowers, mint leaves and flowers, and blue cornflowers. You will also need 15 ml (1 tbsp) orris root powder and 15 drops rose geranium essential oil.

Place the mixture in a polythene bag and seal for 2 weeks, shaking occasionally. To display the finished pot pourri, remove some of the prettiest shells from the bag, then turn the mixture into your container and arrange the shells on the top. If you have any small star fish or sea horses they would look lovely placed on the top as well.

Remove the stalks from all the flowers and leaves, then gently mix together the ingredients in a bowl. Add the orris root powder and mix again. Finally, add the drops of rose geranium essential oil and mix well until all the oil has been absorbed. Put the mixture into a polythene bag and seal well. Leave for 2 weeks, shaking occasionally.

When the pot pourri has matured, shake well before turning it out of the bag into the container of your choice. Place some of the large, more interesting pieces on top of the bowl as a decoration.

Take some fresh roses, carefully pull off the petals and lay them across a wire rack to dry.

Once you have a sufficient quantity of dried rose petals, place them all in a mixing bowl and add a few drops of rose essential oil to intensify the smell.

This gaily coloured pot pourri smells just as good as it looks! You will need the following ingredients: 1 cup dried marigold flowers, 4 or 5 broken cinnamon sticks, 15 ml (1 tbsp) each of cloves, star anise and allspice berries and 30 ml (2 tbsp) dried small green leaves, 15 ml (1 tbsp) orris root powder and 12 drops of cinnamon or allspice essential oil.

Put the rose petal confetti into a clear bag and tie up with ribbons to take to a wedding or give as a wedding gift.

Place the marigolds, spices and leaves in a mixing bowl and, using a metal spoon, mix them together gently. Add the orris root powder and mix it carefully with the other ingredients.

Drop in the oil and mix until it has been absorbed. Place the mixture in a polythene bag and seal. Allow it to mature for 2 weeks, shaking occasionally, then empty it into a suitable container. You can either decorate the pot pourri with pieces of cinnamon and marigolds or with roses that have been air dried or dried in silica gel crystals (see pages 8-9).

This pot pourri can easily be made from garden flowers. The mixture illustrated uses the following ingredients: 30 ml (2 tbsp) each of dried pink larkspur, nigella seed heads, white everlasting daisies, small green leaves, pink roses, red rose petals and lavender. You will also need 30 ml (2 tbsp) orris root powder and 15-20 drops carnation essential oil.

Christmas is a time for exciting smells and this pot pourri would be perfect for the hall or living room to greet your guests. The ingredients used here are: 2 handfuls assorted cones, 1 cup smallish nuts, 6 cinnamon sticks, 1 cup peeled root ginger, 1 handful dried orange peel, 15 ml (1 tbsp) star anise, 2 or 3 cracked nutmegs and some gold sprayed nigella seed heads or cones.

Place all the flowers in a mixing bowl and mix gently. Add the orris root powder and carnation oil and mix thoroughly with a metal spoon.

Mix all the above ingredients together, except the gold seed heads or cones, and add 30 ml (2 tbsp) orris root powder. Then add 10 drops allspice oil, 10 drops ginger oil and 15 drops sweet orange essential oil. Mix all these in thoroughly with a metal spoon.

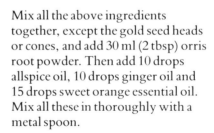

Put the mixture into a polythene bag and seal. Leave for 2 weeks, shaking the bag occasionally. When the pot pourri has matured, turn it out into the container you have chosen and decorate the top with carnations dried in silica gel crystals (see page 9) or any other flower of your choice.

Place the mixture in a polythene bag and seal for 2 weeks, giving the bag a shake occasionally. Once the mixture is ready, place in a suitably festive container and decorate the top with the gilded nigella seed heads or cones and place in position. If it is placed near a fire or warm radiator, the heat will encourage the perfume to waft around the room.

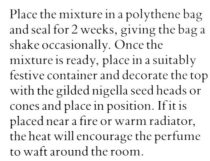

SACHETS, PILLOWS AND POMANDERS

C ut out a square of lace fabric slightly larger than the diameter of your embroidery hoop. You will also need some brightly coloured pot pourri, ribbons and lace.

Stretch the square of lace fabric across the embroidery hoop and secure it.

Turn the hoop over and fill with pot pourri. Trim any excess lace from the edge of the hoop.

Using a hot glue gun, glue a circle of lace to the back of the hoop and trim to fit exactly. Glue satin ribbon around the edge of the embroidery hoop and glue ready-gathered lace around the back of the frame. Tie a length of ribbon to the screw attachment on the hoop for hanging and then trim with dried flowers and a ribbon bow, using the glue gun to secure them.

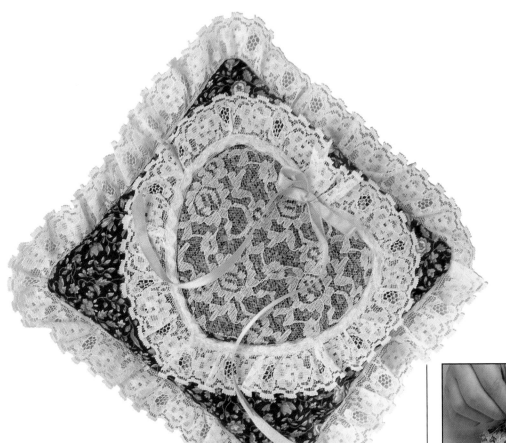

Back, with the lace, the piece of cotton fabric with the heart cut out of it.

Cut out 2 pieces of cotton fabric and one piece of lace, all about 18 cm (7 in) square. You will also need some dried lavender flowers and leaves, and some dried herbs.

Trim the right side of the cut-out heart shape with some ready-gathered lace. Place the 2 pieces of cotton fabric right sides together and sew around 3 of the sides. Leave the fourth side open for filling. Turn the sachet the right side out and then fill with dried lavender flowers, leaves and herbs.

Cut out a heart shape, using the template on page 92, from the middle of one of the pieces of cotton fabric.

Neatly sew along the open edge to finish the sachet and then trim with more of the ready-gathered lace used on the heart shape. Finally, sew or glue on a small bow to decorate the heart.

Cut out 2 rectangles of muslin, or another fine fabric, to the required size. You will also need some pot pourri scented with the essential oil of your choice.

Machine-stitch 3 sides of the rectangle, leaving the fourth side open for turning.

Cut out a 25 cm (10 in) circle of lace fabric and 20.5 cm (8 in) circle of cotton or other pretty fabric. You will also need a small teddy or doll and some pot pourri.

Turn the muslin sachet right sides out and fill with the pot pourri.

Stitch the cotton fabric to the lace to line it. Place lace side down and put some polyester wadding on top. Place the teddy on the wadding and add some pot pourri.

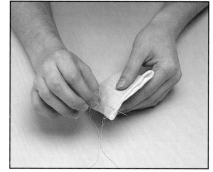

Turn under the raw edges of the sachet and oversew by hand. The satchet can be opened and filled with more pot pourri when the existing mixture loses its scent. You can place the sachet inside the oven gloves (see page 59), herbal hot mat (see page 60), tea cosy (see page 61) or inside cushions.

Gather up the lace and fasten off firmly. Decorate the bear as shown with lace, beads and ribbon. There are many variations at this point; use whatever you happen to have handy to add to the finished effect. These trimmings can be sewn on or attached with a hot glue gun.

These were referred to as sweet bags in the past because of their sweet smell – nothing to do with the edible variety of sweets! Take one cotton lawn, lace-edged handkerchief and place 15 ml (1 tbsp) strongly scented pot pourri in the centre.

Gather up the edges of the handkerchief so that they are all of equal length and secure the bundle with a small elastic band.

Tie a narrow ribbon around the neck and decorate the bag by adding some pink rosebuds or other flowers, using a hot glue gun.

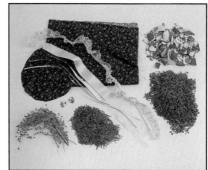

Cut out a rectangle of fabric 50 x 27.5 cm (20 x 11in) and a second circular piece about 12.5 cm (5 in) in diameter. You will also need lace and wide and narrow ribbons. For the filling, collect some dried lavender, rosemary, orange peel and wormwood – all of which will help to scent and protect your linen.

Stitch the lace to one long end of the fabric, adding a ribbon loop at the centre. Sew the wide ribbon about 5 cm (2 in) in from the lace edge, at the top and bottom so ribbon can be threaded through it. Fold the material in half, right sides inwards, and sew the 2 short sides together. Gather the fabric at the base edge to fit it onto the wrong side of the fabric circle. Stitch the circle to the base.

Turn the bag the right way out. Make neat holes where the wide ribbon is joined at the seams, and at the front of the bag. Thread some narrow ribbon through the wide ribbon at the top of the bag. Fill the bag with the rosemary mixture, pull the ribbon to close it and tie the ribbon in a bow. Decorate, if wished, with small ribbon roses and more ribbon.

Collect together some dried orange peel, small dried green leaves, 10 ml (2 tsp) orris root powder and some bergamot essential oil. You will also need a 25-27.5 cm (10-11 in) circle of lace fabric edged with pre-gathered lace and some narrow ribbon.

In a bowl, mix together the orange peel, leaves, orris root powder and a few drops of bergamot oil. Make sure all the oil is absorbed by the powder and other ingredients.

Thread the narrow ribbon all around the edge of the lace circle, about 2.5 cm (1 in) in from the edge.

Pull the ribbon to gather the edges into a bag shape and fill with pot pourri. Gather the ribbon tightly to secure the pot pourri in the sachet and tie in a firm bow.

M ix together a handful of dried tulip petals, marigolds, poppies and rose petals and add 15 ml (1 tbsp) orris root powder.

Add 20 drops of any floral essential oil of your choice and mix well. Cut out 2 pieces of calico 45 cm (18 in) square and join them together, leaving a small gap for filling.

Turn the pillow the right side out, then fill with a mixture of scented pot pourri and polyester cushion filling. Sew along the gap to close the pillow. Cut out 2 pieces of cotton fabric 45 cm (18 in) square, stitch some ribbon and lace across the corners of one piece and then edge the same piece with some cream Cluny lace or any other lace of your choice.

Assuming your fabric to be 1.3 m (4 ft) wide, cut 3 strips 10 cm (4 in) wide and join together along the short edges to make the frill. Edge with lace and gather to fit the pillow. Stitch it to the decorated piece, then cover the seam with lace. Join the 2 pieces together with their right sides facing, leaving a gap for turning. Turn and press. Place the calico pillow inside and sew up the gap.

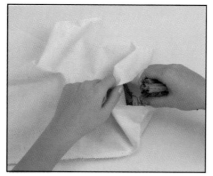

F or this cushion you will need some dried rosemary, dried mint leaves, orris root powder, broken cinnamon sticks and any essential oil of your choice. Quantities will depend upon the size of cushion you wish to make. You will also need some pretty cotton or polyester fabric, some unbleached calico for the liner and some ribbon or lace for decoration.

Make a plain bag slightly smaller than the size of cushion you require using the calico and fill with the mixture of herbs and orris root powder with added drops of essential oil. Cut out 2 pieces of the cotton or polyester material the size you require for the cushion.

Cut out 10 cm (4 in) strips of the same fabric and join them together to make a frill. Hem one edge.

Place the 2 pieces of cushion fabric right sides together, and pin the raw edge of the frill around 3 sides of the cushion between the 2 pieces of fabric, gathering the frill as you pin. Leave a short side open for turning, pinning the frill to what will be the top side of the cushion.

Sew the frill and fabric together either by hand or machine. Turn the cushion the right way out, place the calico bag inside, then sew up the fourth side. Trim the cushion with ribbon and/or lace as required.

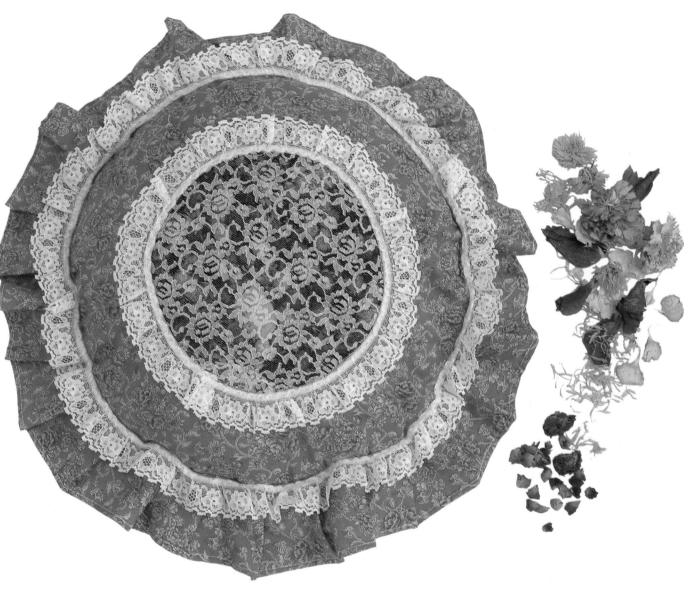

For the cushion filling you need a collection of dried flower petals or some ready-made pot pourri, mixed with 30 ml (2 tbsp) orris root powder. The cushion takes two 37.5 cm (15 in) circles of cotton fabric, a 22.5 cm (9 in) circle of lace fabric and enough pre-gathered lace to trim the cushion and the lace centre. The trimmings from the cotton fabric can be used for the frill.

Cut a 20 cm (8 in) wide hole from the centre of one piece of the cotton fabric.

Back this hole with the circle of lace fabric, pinning and then sewing it on firmly.

Edge this cut-out section with pre-gathered lace, then edge this piece of the cotton fabric with more lace. Sew 10 cm (4 in) strips of the cotton fabric together to make a frill. With right sides together, sew the 2 cushion pieces together with the frill between them, leaving a gap. Turn the right way out, pour in the flower petals, then sew up the gap.

In a bowl, mix together 55 g (2 oz) each of dried rosemary, lavender and wormwood.

Add to the mixture 25 g (1 oz/¼ cup) orris root powder, 2 crushed cinnamon sticks and 10 ml (2 tsp) cloves and mix well.

This pillow is made from unbleached calico. You will also need some cotton lace to trim the pillow and some dried hop flowers. Cut 2 pieces of calico and pin them together with the lace edging between them. Pin around 3 of the 4 sides, leaving one open to fill with hops. On the fourth side, pin and then sew the lace to what will be the top side of the pillow.

Add 3 drops lavender essential oil and 1 drop rosemary essential oil. Mix well, then place 15 ml (1 tbsp) of the mixture in the centre of a lace-edged handkerchief. Gather up the sides and secure with a small elastic band. Repeat to make as many as you need. Hang in wardrobes or a linen cupboard with a loop of ribbon.

Turn the pillow the right way out and fill well with hop flowers, shaking them down as you put them into the pillow. Sew up the fourth side.

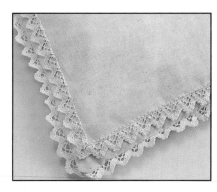

Add an extra row of lace to decorate the pillow, as shown here, if wished. To use, tuck this sleep pillow inside your normal pillow case.

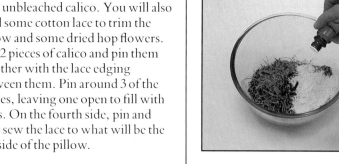

This little rosebud ball is simply lovely. The rosebuds can be obtained from a specialist dried flower supplier or from a shop that sells loose pot pourri. You will need 3 or 4 handfuls of rosebuds, a 7.5 cm (3 in) dried flower foam ball, three 15 cm (6 in) lengths of medium gauge florist's wire, 30–35 cm (12–14 in) lengths of ribbon and one of lace.

These apple pomanders look lovely piled in a bowl, either amongst fresh fruit or with nuts, or with a selection of other pomanders. You can also make pomanders from lemons, oranges and limes. If you want to hang it up, fix a length of ribbon round the apple and make it into a loop. Take a fresh apple and use a knitting needle to make small holes in it.

Make a loop with the length of lace and wrap a wire around the ends, leaving a leg that is at least 10 cm (4 in) long. Push this wire straight through the foam ball and out the other side. Bend the end over to make a hook and push it back up into the foam to secure it in place. The ribbons can then be wired in the same way, but with shorter legs, and just pushed into the ball.

Fill the holes with whole cloves, then continue in this way until you have covered the entire apple.

Take a rosebud and, starting near the point where the ribbon meets the foam ball, press the short stem into the foam. Continue to press in rosebuds, either in a random pattern or in straight lines, until the ball is completely covered. Take care to sort out the rosebuds first, so you use only the best shapes, sizes and colours.

Roll the finished apple or several apples in a polythene bag containing 15 ml (1 tbsp) orris root powder and 15 ml (1 tbsp) mixed powdered spices, then place the apple pomanders to dry on a warm radiator or in an airing cupboard for several weeks until they are completely dry.

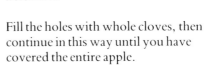

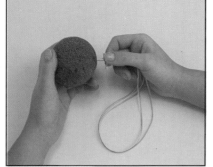

Cover the foam ball with sea lavender, or *Statice dumosa*.

Ⓜ️ake 2 long loops with toning colour ribbons and wrap some florist's wire around the base of the loops, leaving a long enough leg to pass through a 7 cm (2¾ in) or 9 cm (3½ in) dried flower foam ball.

Push the wire through the ball, until the base of each loop has disappeared. Trim the wire to within 1 cm (½ in) of the ball and bend that 1 cm (½ in) back on itself to disappear inside the foam.

Place other dried flowers, such as achillea or helichrysum, at random over the ball. You can also add wired pearl loops or more ribbon loops if you like.

Using a favourite essential oil or pot pourri oil, place a few drops deep into the dried flowers to add a finishing touch.

BEAUTY PREPARATIONS

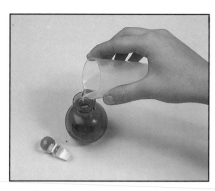

P̶our 75 ml (2½ fl oz/⅓ cup) almond oil into a pretty bottle or container.

Mix together 15 ml (1 tbsp) neroli (orange blossom) essential oil and 5 ml (1 tsp) rose essential oil and add to the bottle.

Shake the bottle well, label clearly and then leave for 2 weeks before using in your bath. Use about 15 ml (1 tbsp) in a bath, adding it to the filled bath.

I̶n a small jug, mix together 150 ml (5 fl oz/⅔ cup) any organic washing up liquid, and 150 ml (5 fl oz/⅔ cup) distilled water.

Add 5 ml (1 tsp) rose geranium essential oil to this mixture and stir well.

Add 3 drops of pink food colouring, or more if you want a stronger colour, and mix through the liquid. Decant the bubble bath into an attractive container which can be decorated with ribbons or flowers if it is to be given as a gift. Use 15 ml (1 tbsp) in a bath, adding it to the running water.

In a bowl, mix together 45 g (1½ oz) dried marjoram, 45 g (1½ oz) dried rosemary, 30 ml (2 tbsp) porridge oats and 15 g (1 tbsp) dried chopped orange peel.

Cut out several 22.5 cm (9 in) circles of calico and place about 20 ml (2 dessertspoons) of the herb mixture in the centre of each one. Gather up the material to make a bag and secure each one with a small elastic band.

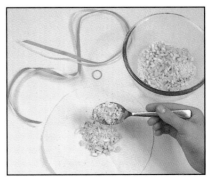

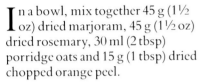

Tie long pieces of ribbon around the neck of each bundle, both to decorate and to attach the bag to the bath taps. The bag should be fixed to the taps before you run your bath, so the water runs through the herbal mixture.

Thickly peel 1 or 2 lemons, until you have about 15 g (½ oz) of peel, then chop it roughly. You also need peeled and chopped fresh root ginger, 25 g (1 oz/⅓ cup) porridge oats and some lily of the valley essential oil.

In a bowl, combine all the ingredients, adding 2–3 drops of the lily of the valley oil. Stir well to ensure all the ingredients are well mixed.

Cut out several 25 cm (10 in) circles of calico and place about 20 ml (2 dessertspoons) of the mixture in the centre of each circle. Gather up the material to make a bag and secure with a small elastic band. Tie long pieces of ribbon around the neck of each bundle, both to decorate and to attach the bag to the bath taps, so the water runs through the mixture.

Put 450 ml (16 fl oz/2 cups) lavender flowers and leaves in a small saucepan and add 300 ml (10 fl oz/ 1¼ cups) water.

Put 115 ml (4 fl oz/½ cup) castor oil in a jug and add 10 drops honeysuckle perfume or pot pourri oil. Mix well.

Heat to simmering point and then simmer gently for about 5 minutes, stirring occasionally.

Choose some suitable containers – whether you are making this as a gift or for yourself, it always looks much better in an attractive container. Pour the mixture into the containers.

Let the contents of the pan cool and then strain through a fine sieve into a jug. Pour the liquid into a bottle. When a soothing foot bath is required, add half the bottle to a bowl of warm water and soak the feet well.

Seal well and label. About 5 ml (1 tsp) is sufficient for an average bath. Add it to the filled bath.

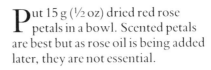

Put 15 g (½ oz) dried red rose petals in a bowl. Scented petals are best but as rose oil is being added later, they are not essential.

Pour 300 ml (10 fl oz/1¼ cups) boiling water over the petals and stir well. Leave to infuse for roughly 2 hours.

Put 45 ml (3 tbsp) bicarbonate of soda in a bowl and add 12 drops sweet orange or neroli (orange blossom) essential oil and 6 drops strawberry perfume or pot pourri oil. Mix well together.

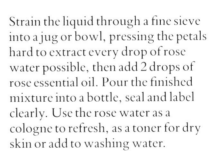

Strain the liquid through a fine sieve into a jug or bowl, pressing the petals hard to extract every drop of rose water possible, then add 2 drops of rose essential oil. Pour the finished mixture into a bottle, seal and label clearly. Use the rose water as a cologne to refresh, as a toner for dry skin or add to washing water.

Add some pink food colouring – 3 drops should be ample, depending on the depth of colour required.

Mix the food colouring in well, which takes quite a while and needs to be done very thoroughly. Pour the salts into a clear jar and decorate with a pink ribbon. Add about 15 ml (1 tbsp) to a hot bath.

This is a delicious after-bath cologne. You will need some cheap vodka, distilled water, dried orange peel, cloves, a fresh rose and a carnation, and bergamot essential oil.

Take a fresh rose and a fresh carnation and strip off the petals, placing them in a screw-top jar. Pour over 115 ml (4 fl oz/½ cup) cheap vodka. Screw on the top, shake well and leave on a sunny windowsill for about 1 week.

Measure 45 ml (3 tbsp) dried orange peel and 5 ml (1 tsp) cloves into a bowl and pour over 350 ml (12 fl oz/ 1½ cups) boiling distilled water. Leave to stand for 5–6 hours.

Strain both the flower and vodka mixture and the orange and clove mixture through a fine sieve into a bowl or jug.

Check for clarity – the liquid may need straining through a finer sieve to clear it completely. Add 3 drops bergamot essential oil and stir well. Pour the liquid into a bottle and keep in the refrigerator or other cool place. Use as an after-bath cologne.

P lace 15 ml (1 tbsp) fresh mint leaves in a bowl with 15 ml (1 tbsp) rosemary leaves and pour over 50 ml (2 fl oz/¼ cup) cheap vodka.

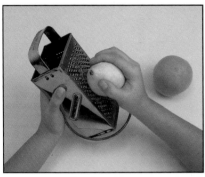

Carefully grate the peel from 1 orange and 1 lemon, removing as much as possible.

Add the orange and lemon peel to the mint, rosemary and vodka mixture.

Add 115 ml (4 fl oz/½ cup) rose water and mix all the ingredients together.

Leave the mixture for about 1 week, stirring vigorously every day. Carefully strain the liquid through a sieve and then pour into a bottle. Keep in a cool place and use as a cologne or in bath water.

Pour 150 ml (5 fl oz/⅔ cup) cheap vodka into a large perfume bottle or 2 small bottles.

Add 6 drops neroli (orange blossom) essential oil and 2 drops coriander essential oil to the vodka.

Shake the bottle or bottles very vigorously. Leave to stand for 1–2 weeks, then check the fragrance – if you wish to alter the balance of the ingredients, add a drop more of whichever fragrance you require.

Put 30 ml (2 tbsp) dried rosemary in a heatproof bowl. Heat 200 ml (7 fl oz/¾ cup) distilled water and pour over the dried rosemary. Leave to infuse for 5–6 hours.

Add 5 ml (1 tsp) almond oil and 2 drops rosemary essential oil to the mixture.

Whisk gently until all the ingredients are well mixed. Then strain the liquid through a fine sieve and pour into a bottle. Keep in a cool place.

Put 45 ml (3 tbsp) dried strawberry leaves in a heatproof bowl. Bring just over 100 ml (3½ fl oz/⅓ cup) distilled water to the boil, then pour over the strawberry leaves. Leave to infuse for 4–5 hours.

Heat 115 ml (4 fl oz/½ cup) rose water in a bowl set over a saucepan of simmering water. When hot, add 5 ml (1 tsp) borax.

Stir very gently until the borax has completely dissolved.

Remove the bowl from the heat. Strain the liquid away from the strawberry leaves through a sieve into the rose water and borax mixture.

Pour the liquid into a suitable bottle. This aftershave works best if it is kept cool or, better still, stored in the refrigerator before and after use.

   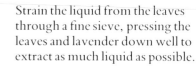

Combine 250 ml (9 fl oz/1 cup) cider vinegar and 250 ml (9 fl oz/ 1 cup) water in a saucepan and heat gently – do not boil.

Remove from the heat and add 15 ml (1 tbsp) dried basil and 15 ml (1 tbsp) dried mint. Leave to infuse for 5-6 hours.

Combine 550 ml (20 fl oz/2½ cups) cider vinegar with the same quantity of water in a saucepan and heat to boiling point. Put 25 g (1 oz) lavender flowers and 85 g (3 oz) geranium leaves in a heatproof bowl, pour over the boiling liquid and leave to infuse for 10-12 hours.

Strain the liquid from the leaves through a fine sieve, pressing the leaves and lavender down well to extract as much liquid as possible.

Strain the mixture through a fine sieve and pour into a bottle. Use in the bath – about a cupful for an average bath.

Add 2 drops lavender essential oil and 2 drops rose geranium essential oil and mix gently. Pour into bottles. Use in the bath – about a cupful for an average bath.

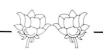

This eyebath used cold from the refrigerator will calm sore eyes and bring a sparkle back to tired eyes. You need 7 g (¼ oz) dried cornflowers and 200 ml (7 fl oz/scant 1 cup) distilled water.

For this mask you must use dried marigold petals (any variety) and a good quality plain yoghurt, made from either sheep's or cow's milk. Put 90 ml (6 tbsp) dried marigold petals in a bowl. Heat 45 ml (3 tbsp) distilled water and then pour it over the petals.

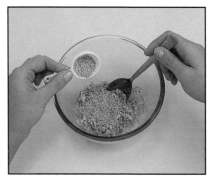

Put the cornflowers in a heatproof bowl. Bring the distilled water to the boil and pour it over the cornflowers. Leave to infuse for 1 hour.

Add 60 ml (4 tbsp) oatmeal and 15 ml (1 tbsp) granulated lecithin. Stir the mixture very vigorously.

Strain carefully through a fine sieve into a jug or bottle. Chill in the refrigerator. To refresh eyes, soak pads of cotton wool with this mixture, place on closed eyes and rest for 15-20 minutes. This mix should be used fresh and only stored for a maximum of 24 hours in the refrigerator.

Add 60 ml (4 tbsp) plain yoghurt and mix in well. The mask should be applied to your face whilst it is still warm. Leave the mask on for 20-30 minutes and then carefully rinse it off with lukewarm water.

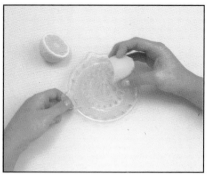

Squeeze half a lemon and measure out 5 ml (1 tsp) of juice. Chop 1 cucumber into cubes.

Put the egg whites in a food processor or blender with 3 ice cubes, the lemon juice, chopped cucumber, 5 ml (1 tsp) vodka and 4 drops peppermint essential oil. Blend until a smooth paste is formed.

This face mask is good for oily skins. In a bowl, whisk 2 egg whites until they are standing in soft peaks.

To use, apply the mixture to your face, leave for 5-10 minutes, then rinse off carefully. Any remaining mixture may be stored in the refrigerator for a day or so.

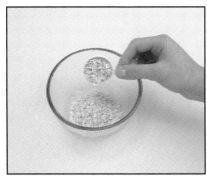

Measure 4.5 ml (3 tbsp) porridge oats into a bowl. If you prefer a finer mask, process the porridge oats in a food processor or blender for a few seconds first.

Add 15-30 ml (1-2 tbsp) rose water, depending on the preferred consistency, working the mixture into a paste.

Add 2 drops rose essential oil and mix in thoroughly. To use, apply to the face and leave for 15 minutes, then rinse off gently. Apply a gentle toner to close the pores. This is a good refining mask.

Put 15 ml (1 tbsp) dried raspberry leaves with the same quantity of strawberry leaves and dried orange peel in a large bowl.

Pour over 2 litres (70 fl oz/9 cups) boiling water.

Add 1-2 drops sweet orange or neroli (orange blossom) essential oil. Stir well until all the ingredients are mixed together. To use, place a towel over your head, lower your face until it is just above the bowl and breathe in the vapour. Stay under the towel for about 10 minutes, then use a gentle astringent to close the pores.

I n a bowl, mix together 45 ml
(3 tbsp) dried red rose petals, 15 ml
(1 tbsp) dried raspberry leaves and
5 ml (1 tsp) camomile flowers.

Heat 150 ml (5 fl oz/⅔ cup) distilled
water with 45 ml (3 tbsp) cider
vinegar but do not allow it to boil.
Pour the hot liquid over the flowers
and leaves.

Stir the mixture well and leave to
cool. When cold, cover with cling
film and leave in the refrigerator for
1 week.

Strain the liquid away from the
petals through a fine sieve into a
bowl.

In a small bowl, mix together 5 ml
(1 tsp) borax and 200 ml (7 fl oz/
¾ cup) rose water. Add to the rose
and raspberry liquid and mix really
well. Then pour into a bottle and
label clearly. This facial splash feels
nicest if used straight from the
refrigerator.

Collect some roses fresh from the garden or, if necessary, buy some from a good florist, checking that they have not been sprayed with chemicals. You will also need 45 ml (3 tbsp) porridge oats, 15 ml (1 tbsp) single (light) cream, 30 ml (2 tbsp) almond oil and some rose water.

Remove the petals from the roses and chop them finely or process them in a food processor. Then fill a measuring jug with the petals, packing them down quite hard until you reach the 200 ml (7 fl oz/¾ cup) level.

Add the porridge oats, then chop the mixture even more finely or re-process in the food processor.

Place the chopped ingredients in a bowl and add the single (light) cream and almond oil. Mix these in thoroughly.

Finally, add a little rose water until the mixture is a workable paste. To use, apply the mask and leave on the face for 20-30 minutes whilst you relax, then gently rinse off.

Melt 15 ml (1 tbsp) lanolin in a bowl set over a saucepan with 2.5-5 cm (1-2 in) of simmering water in it.

Once the lanolin has melted, remove from the heat and add 175 ml (6 fl oz/ ¾ cup) almond oil and mix gently.

Add 250 ml (9 fl oz/1 cup) dried elderflowers and stir in. Place the bowl and pan of hot water back on the heat and let the water simmer very gently for about 20 minutes.

Strain the mixture through a sieve, then pour it into a jar and let it cool. This is an excellent all-purpose hand or body cream.

Put 10 ml (2 tsp) dried elderflowers in a heatproof bowl. Heat 1 litre (35 fl oz/4½ cups) distilled water and pour it over the dried elderflowers. Cover with cling film and leave to infuse for about 3-4 hours.

Strain the liquid away from the flowers through a fine sieve. Warm 30 ml (2 tbsp) white vinegar and dissolve 1.25 ml (¼ tsp) borax in the vinegar.

This lotion is ideal for the area around the eyes. It is gentle enough for dry skin and helps to tighten the areas of the face most prone to wrinkles. You need 30 ml (2 tbsp) dried poppy petals, 15 ml (1 tbsp) dried cornflowers, 300 ml (10 fl oz/1¼ cups) distilled water and a suitable bottle or container and some ribbon.

Add the vinegar and borax mixture to the elderflower liquid and mix well. Pour into a bottle and keep in a cool place – it is best used straight from the refrigerator and is ideal for oily skins.

Place the poppy petals and cornflowers in a small saucepan and add the distilled water. Bring to the boil and then turn off the heat. Allow the petals to infuse for 30-40 minutes.

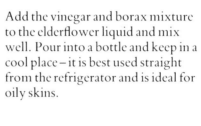

Strain the infusion through a fine sieve or tea strainer into a jug. Pour the liquid from the jug into your chosen bottle or bottles and seal. Use this mixture by applying it, on a pad of cotton wool, to the face and neck both night and morning. It is best kept in the refrigerator, as this helps to preserve the mixture and also makes the lotion feel extra invigorating when it is applied.

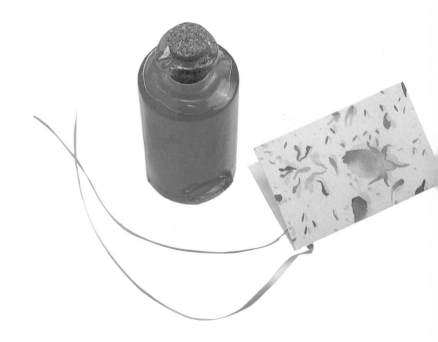

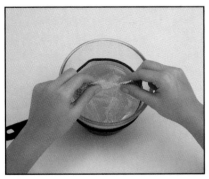

Put 215 ml (7½ fl oz/¾ cup plus 8 tsp) almond oil in a heatproof bowl set over a saucepan of simmering water, add 30 ml (2 tbsp) beeswax and stir until melted.

Add 15 ml (1 tbsp) glycerine to the mixture and stir well.

Warm 175 ml (6 fl oz/¾ cup) rose water, add 5 ml (1 tsp) borax and stir until dissolved, then add to the beeswax mixture.

Remove the bowl of beeswax mixture from the saucepan and whisk really well until the mixture has cooled. Spoon into a jar and keep this mixture in the refrigerator.

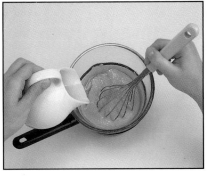

Put 45 ml (3 tbsp) lanolin and 115 ml (4 fl oz/½ cup) beeswax in a heatproof bowl set over a saucepan with 2.5-5 cm (1-2 in) simmering water in it. Stir until the beeswax has melted.

Add 175 ml (6 fl oz/¾ cup) almond oil and whisk all the ingredients together.

Add 60 ml (4 tbsp) distilled water, a little at a time, whisking constantly.

Remove the bowl from the saucepan and whisk in 10 drops lavender essential oil, 10 drops sweet orange essential oil, 5 drops rosemary essential oil and 5 drops bergamot essential oil. Spoon into suitable containers and keep cool.

Put 60 ml (4 tbsp) crushed rosehips in a heatproof bowl. In a small saucepan, bring 200 ml (7 fl oz/ ¾ cup) distilled water to the boil. Pour over the rosehips and leave to infuse for 1-2 hours.

Strain the liquid away from the rosehips by pouring it through some muslin or cheesecloth into another bowl.

Heat 20 ml (4 tsp) almond oil in a bowl set over a saucepan with 2.5-5 cm (1-2 in) simmering water in the bottom. Add 10 ml (2 tsp) granulated lecithin and stir well until the granules have dissolved.

Add 5 ml (1 tsp) cider vinegar to the rosehip water. Set the bowl over a saucepan of simmering water and heat gently almost to boiling point – do not allow to boil.

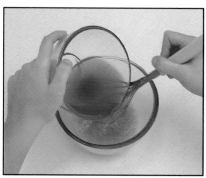

Mix all the ingredients together and whisk well until they have cooled. Pour the lotion into a bottle and keep in the refrigerator.

Melt 5 ml (1 tsp) beeswax with 15 ml (1 tbsp) lanolin and 90 ml (6 tbsp) almond oil in a bowl set over a saucepan of simmering water. Stir gently while they are melting.

Heat 45 ml (3 tbsp) distilled water with 60 ml (4 tbsp) carrot juice in a small saucepan. Add 2.5 ml (½ tsp) borax and dissolve well.

This is a wonderfully rich and nourishing cream that is ideal for softening dry skin at night. You need 10 ml (2 tsp) lanolin, 10 ml (2 tsp) beeswax (or some small pieces from a sheet), 20 ml (4 tsp) almond oil, 15 ml (3 tsp) distilled water, a pinch of borax, 4 capsules wheatgerm oil and 3-4 drops neroli (orange blossom) essential oil. Any container with a tight-fitting lid is suitable.

Add 30 ml (2 tbsp) glycerine to the beeswax and oil mixture and stir well. Remove the bowl from the saucepan and add the carrot juice mixture to the oil mixture, whisking until the cream has cooled down. Add 3 drops sweet orange essential oil to the cream, then spoon into a jar with a tight-fitting lid.

Put the lanolin, beeswax and almond oil in a bowl and place over a saucepan containing 2.5-5 cm (1-2 in) of water. Heat the water and gently melt the ingredients, stirring carefully.

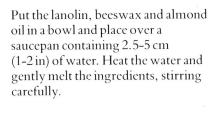

Heat the distilled water in a separate pan, then pour it over the borax to dissolve it and pour into the oil mixture. Stir well, then pierce the capsules of wheatgerm oil and add the contents to the cream. Add the neroli essential oil and mix in thoroughly. Spoon into a container before the mixture becomes too cool and sets. This cream should be used nightly for the best results.

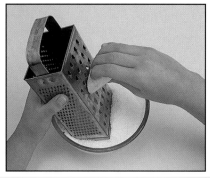

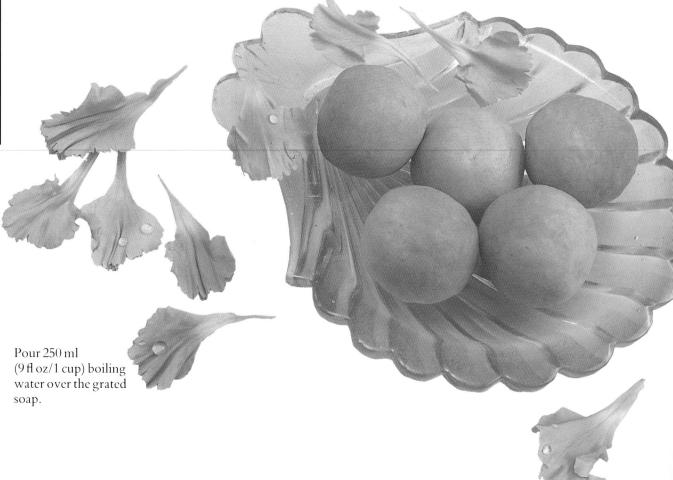

G rate 300 g (10 oz) plain unscented soap into a mixing bowl.

Pour 250 ml (9 fl oz/1 cup) boiling water over the grated soap.

Add 4 drops pink food colouring, 5 drops carnation essential oil and 1 drop clove essential oil.

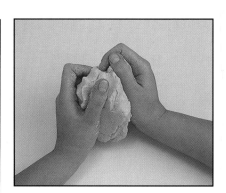

Mix really thoroughly, using a metal spoon, and leave to harden.

Once the soap has hardened, break off small pieces, the size of a table tennis ball.

Roll into balls of an even size and leave to become even harder. When they are really hard, polish with a piece of cotton wool dipped in carnation essential oil.

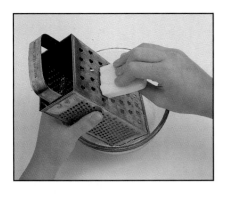

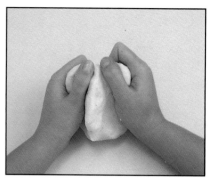

Grate 1 large or 2 small bars of plain unscented soap into a bowl.

Heat 55 ml (2 fl oz/¼ cup) rose water and pour over the grated soap.

Add 2 drops grapefruit essential oil and 2 drops rose geranium essential oil and some lemon yellow food colouring, if desired. Mix in thoroughly.

Let the mixture stand for 1-2 days, then divide into even-sized pieces.

Roll the pieces into smooth balls, allow them to dry thoroughly and then polish them with a piece of cotton wool dipped in rose water.

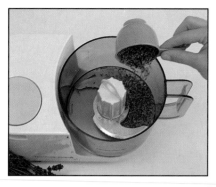

Put 75 ml (5 tbsp) lavender flowers in a food processor or blender with 30 ml (2 tbsp) dried chopped mixed herbs and process to a powder. This is quite a lengthy process but needs to be done thoroughly.

In a bowl, combine 75 ml (5 tbsp) precipitated chalk, 30 ml (2 tbsp) rice flour and 45 ml (3 tbsp) cornflour.

Add the powdered lavender flowers and powdered mixed herbs.

Finally, add 15 ml (1 tbsp) lavender essential oil and mix all the ingredients thoroughly before transferring to a suitable container.

P
ut 115 g (4 oz) camomile flowers in a heatproof bowl. Heat 550 ml (20 fl oz/2½ cups) water to boiling point and pour over the camomile flowers. Leave to infuse for 2 hours.

I
n a bowl, mix together 25 g (1 oz/ ¼ cup) orris root powder with 85 g (3 oz/¾ cup) plain talcum powder.

 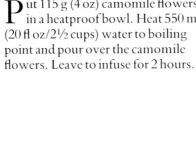

Strain the liquid away from the flowers into a bowl through a fine sieve.

Add 2 drops rosemary essential oil and 2 drops lemon essential oil. Stir well with a metal spoon.

Pour the camomile liquid into a jug, passing it through some muslin to strain off any tiny pieces of camomile left behind. Pour into a pretty container and use as a final rinse when washing blonde hair.

Once the oils have been well mixed in, use as a freshener between shampoos. Rub a small quantity into the hair and then brush out well with a bristle brush.

P̶ut 115 g (4 oz) elderberries in a bowl and crush them slightly.

Bring 550 ml (20 fl oz/2½ cups) water to boiling point and pour over the elderberries.

Stir the mixture and leave to infuse for approximately 2 hours.

Strain off the liquid and pour into a bottle. Used as a final rinse for grey hair, it imparts a slight blue/grey tone.

FOR THE HOME

Collect some scented rose petals from the garden and wash them well. Dry carefully with tissues and lay out on a cake cooling rack to dry.

Finely chop some dried marigold flowers. You will need 20 ml (2 dessertspoons) for a 225 g (8 oz) pot of mustard. It is best to use a strong, grainy mustard.

Once they are dry, store them in the box or container you wish to give them in as a present and gradually add to them.

Mix the chopped marigolds into the mustard, making sure they are well distributed.

Decorate the box or container with some dried flowers, ribbon and perhaps a label. To make rose petal tea, pour 300 ml (½ pint) boiling water over 10 ml (1 dessertspoon) rose petals and allow to stand, then strain well. Elderflowers can be used instead of rose petals if you prefer.

Spoon the marigold mustard into a sealable container, seal it, then decorate with a suitable bow or other decoration. This mustard is excellent with cold pork.

Choose an attractive container to fill with oil. Measure how much oil it will hold, then add 30 ml (2 tbsp) dried rose petals per 600 ml (1 pint) oil.

Using a funnel, pour the oil – sunflower or rapeseed works well – over the rose petals. Leave to mature for a couple of days, shaking occasionally.

Decorate the container before giving it as a present, using some dainty rose-coloured ribbon.

Fill the base of a pretty glass container with dried carnation heads.

Add white wine or cider vinegar, filling the container to the top.

Seal the top and then decorate the container with some pretty ribbons.

Y ou will need some dried lavender, a funnel, white wine or cider vinegar, a suitable container and some ribbon.

Place some lavender stalks in the container with their heads pointing downwards. Fill up the container with the vinegar.

Seal the top and then decorate the bottle with a spray of lavender and some ribbons.

W arm a pot of runny honey, plus a handful of lavender flowers, in a heatproof bowl over a saucepan of gently simmering water. Do not allow the honey to boil, just gently warm it through with the lavender for about 15 minutes.

Strain the honey through a fine sieve and discard the lavender flowers.

Pour the honey into an attractive container and place a sprig of lavender in the top. Seal the container and then decorate it with a small bunch of lavender and some ribbons.

You will need 2 pieces of washable fabric 1m (40 in) long by 20.5 cm (8 in) wide, 2 pieces of the same fabric measuring 15 x 10 cm (6 x 4 in) and some muslin for the sachets. The herb pot pourri mixture is made from a handful of each of the following: dried mint, marjoram, wormwood and lavender.

Place the herbs in a bowl and add 15 ml (1 tbsp) orris root powder and 10-15 drops of any herbal essential oil of your choice. Mix well.

Make small muslin sachets about 7.5 x 5 cm (3 x 2 in) and fill with the herbal pot pourri (see page 20). Make 2 small pockets from the 15 x 10 cm (6 x 4 in) pieces of fabric and attach to the wrong side of one of the longer pieces, about 5 cm (2 in) from the ends. Stitch both large pieces of fabric, right sides together, leaving a gap for turning.

Turn right sides out and place an 18 cm (7 in) square of wadding inside each end of the mitt, placing them about 15 cm (6 in) from the ends. Stitch through all the thicknesses to secure the wadding and then turn the ends of the mitt over the wadding and stitch. Sew a loop of ribbon in the centre to hang the oven mitt on a hook and place the herb sachets in the small pockets inside the mitts.

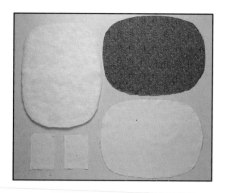
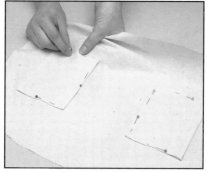

Using the template on page 93, cut out 3 oval shapes 45 cm (18 in) long by 32.5 cm (13 in) wide, one in calico, one in wadding and one in your chosen fabric. Cut out 2 small calico patches to make pockets.

Make the 2 calico pockets and stitch them to the larger piece of calico about 5 cm (2 in) in from the shorter edges.

Stitch the wadding to the other side of the calico. Stitch the main colour fabric to the calico piece, right sides facing, leaving a gap for turning. Turn inside out and press well.

Close the gap and then machine stitch all the way around the mat about 0.5cm (¼ in) in from the edge, to give a decorative finish. Make up a mixture of dried herbal flowers and add 5 ml (1 tsp) orris root powder and a few drops of a herbal essential oil. Fill some muslin sachets (see page 20) and place in the calico pockets under the hot mat.

Fold the strip of cotton fabric lengthwise, with right sides together, and sew along the long edge. Turn right sides out and press flat.

Fold the strip into a loop and sew, at the centre top, onto the right side of one of the pieces of cotton fabric.

Join each piece of calico to its piece of wadding and stitch in place around the edge.

Using the template on page 92, cut out 2 pieces of cotton fabric, 2 pieces of wadding and 2 pieces of calico. You will also need some small pieces of calico and a strip of the cotton fabric.

Stitch the straight edges of the calico pieces and the main fabric pieces together, with right sides together. Open out the calico pieces and the main fabric pieces, and place on top of each other with right sides together. Sew around the edge, leaving a gap for turning in the calico section. Make sure the loop is free and not caught up in the stitching.

Pin and then stitch a small calico pocket to one of the calico shapes, with its open edge facing the curved top of the calico piece.

Turn the cosy right sides out and sew up the gap. Press well, then push the lining inside the main coloured piece. Make up a mixture of aromatic spices, such as cinnamon, nutmeg, star anise and allspice, and mix with 5 ml (1 tsp) orris root powder and some allspice essential oil. Place the mixture in small muslin sachets (see page 20) and put in the calico pocket of the tea cosy.

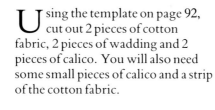

The paper is scented with a strong perfume that is easily made by making up an extra strong sachet of lavender pot pourri and storing it with the paper and envelopes in a box. Lavender, orris root powder and lavender essential oil are combined to make a very potent sachet which soon imparts its fragrance to the contents of the box of writing paper.

You can add a sophisticated touch to all your correspondence by using an ink that has been scented with dried lavender leaves. If you combine this with scented paper and envelopes, your letter will definitely smell delicious! You need a handful of fresh or dried lavender leaves, a bottle of ink and some water.

Mix 30 ml (2 tbsp) dried lavender flowers with 5 ml (1 tsp) orris root powder and add 2 or 3 drops lavender essential oil. Mix all these ingredients together carefully with a metal spoon until the oil and orris root powder are well dispersed amongst the lavender flowers.

Place the lavender leaves in a small saucepan and add approximately 115 ml (4 fl oz/½ cup) water. Bring the water to the boil, then turn the heat down as low as possible and simmer gently for about 30 minutes. Keep an eye on the pan and do not allow the water to evaporate completely. If it gets too low, then add a little more.

Cut out one or more 17.5 cm (7 in) circles of net fabric. Place some or all of the mixture onto the circles and tie the bundle or bundles with wire or ribbons. Place the net bundle or bundles in the box in which you intend to store the paper and envelopes and leave for at least a week, longer if possible, and your letters will have an unforgettable fragrance.

Once the mixture is brown and has become strongly scented, strain off the liquid and discard the lavender leaves. Add a small amount of the liquid to the ink until you are happy with the strength of smell. Here the lavender liquid has been added to lavender-coloured ink to complete the effect.

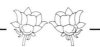

I nto a screw-top jar, pour 150 ml (5 fl oz/⅔ cup) turpentine, 150 ml (5 fl oz/⅔ cup) linseed oil, 85 ml (3 fl oz/⅓ cup) cider vinegar and 85 ml (3 fl oz/⅓ cup) methylated spirits.

F or this insect deterrent you need 685 ml (24 fl oz/3 cups) dried santolina or cotton lavender and 25 g (1 oz) each of cloves, caraway and mace. You will also need 2 or 3 cinnamon sticks.

Add 10-12 drops lavender essential oil to the ingredients in the jar.

Crush the cinnamon sticks into all the other ingredients in a bowl and mix well.

Screw on the lid and shake really thoroughly. Use the mixture to feed wood and always polish off well to give a really good shine to furniture.

Cut out several 25 cm (10 in) circles of calico and fill each one with 15 ml (1 tbsp) of the mixture. Gather up the sides and tie with string or twine. Place in any cupboards or areas that you need to keep insect-free.

In a bowl mix together 250 ml (9 fl oz/1 cup) each of the following: dried lavender flowers, dried thyme, dried oregano and dried orange peel.

Add 1 bottle of white wine (not a special vintage!)

Stir really well until the wine is completely incorporated.

Cover with cling film and leave in a warm room for 1–2 weeks. Then strain the liquid and pour into a bottle. Add 10–15 ml (2–3 tsp) to a final rinse when hand-washing clothes or use as a final rinse for your hair.

DRIED FLOWER DESIGNS

Half-fill a flower pot with plaster of Paris or cement and embed a stick in the middle. The stick should be approximately 35 cm (14 in) long, depending on your required finished height. Once the cement is dry, cover with dry flower foam and arrange some sea lavender to cover the foam.

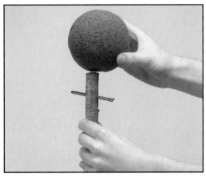

Place a nail through the stick about 2.5 cm (1 in) down from the top and impale a dry flower foam ball onto the stick, with the nail going into the ball.

Cover the ball with sea lavender until the grey foam is barely visible.

Add more dried flowers of your choice in a suitably festive colour, in this case red helichrysum and green *Nigella orientalis*. Make a long loop with some tartan ribbon, attach it to some florist's wire and stick this into the foam ball where the stick (tree trunk) meets the ball.

Finally add some more ribbon loops to the base and some more of the same flowers you used in the top half of the tree.

C hoose an attractive twiggy wreath and, using a hot glue gun, attach a large bow, either centre bottom, to one side or wherever you wish on the wreath.

Glue on some dried hydrangea heads, either part of the way around the wreath or all the way round, depending on your preference.

P lace some dried flower foam in a basket and drop on some essential oil of your choice. Rose always works well.

Add some dried achillea (yarrow) and then some helichrysum heads. Obviously the choice of flowers is yours and can be altered to fit any colour scheme or room.

Fill the basket with dried sea lavender, embedded in the flower foam, and then put in some larkspur.

Add roses and any other flowers you wish, then trim with bows and ribbons to tone in with the colour scheme.

T his wonderful hat is very easy to make at home, especially if you have a hot glue gun: other types of glue are much weaker and more difficult to use. As well as the hat, you will need a bow, some large silk flowers and leaves and some smaller varieties of silk flowers. This design features silk peonies, larkspur and gypsophila, plus some dried sea lavender.

Glue the ribbon bow on to the centre back of the hat and then attach some sea lavender with the hot glue gun. If you wish to use only silk flowers, as opposed to a mixture of silk and dried ingredients, substitute something similar that would make a good base and fill out the design – some pieces of silk hydrangea heads or a larger quantity of the gypsophila are ideal.

When you are happy with the shape of the basic ingredients around the hat, glue on the largest flowers and some leaves. You can either place these in random groups or symmetrically around the brim. Any full, many-petalled flowers are suitable, such as roses, carnations, gardenias or camellias.

Finally, glue on the smaller, more delicate items, which in this case are larkspur and gypsophila. These finer ingredients fill the brim and add a dainty look which balances well with the larger, more dominant flowers. As a final touch you could scent the hat by dropping some essential oil onto the flowers.

This summery combination of poppies, wheat and cornflowers looks wonderful in a rustic wicker hamper. You could use an ordinary basket if a small hamper is not easily available. Fill the hamper with a large piece of dried flower foam.

Cover the foam with dried hydrangea heads to camouflage it. You could use moss or some sea lavender if preferred.

Add some dried wheat, making sure the stems are inserted at pleasing angles and do not all rigidly point towards the sky. This arrangement needs quite a lot of wheat to pad out the display and give a good contrast to the red silk poppies. Alternatively, some dried achillea (yarrow) and dried poppy seed heads can be used, as shown here.

Place some silk poppies in position next and lastly add some silk or dried cornflowers. Add ribbons, or a ribbon bow, if wished.

Choose a basket, then glue a green plastic frog, which holds dried flower foam in place, into the base of the basket. Place a trimmed block of dried flower foam in the basket, impaled on the prongs of the frog. Cover the foam with sea lavender as a base for the other flowers. Then add several bunches of dried lavender: this adds a delightful colour as well as perfume.

Choose a fairly low basket, either circular or oval. Fill with dried flower foam, then take some wheat, place it in a tight circle and stick the stems into the foam, one at a time. It is important to get the bundle of wheat closely packed and fairly even.

Once you have enough wheat in place, tie a ribbon around the bunch, securing it with a double knot so that it does not slip, then tie in a decorative bow. Alternatively, you can knot a piece of ribbon around the stalks and trim it neatly, then glue on a ready-made bow.

Add dried roses of your choice. The ones shown here are a champagne colour and very pretty, but you could also use pink or peach. Roses are well worth drying yourself as they are expensive to buy.

Make double loops with some pretty ribbon and wire the base of each loop. Secure these loops either side of the handles, as a finishing touch.

Cover the rest of the foam with dried hydrangea heads so that they form a circle around the wheat. Dried hydrangeas come in many shades, often greens and burgundies, but it is possible to dry the paler blues and pinks.

C ollect together the flowers of your choice to include in your bouquet. Lay out the longest ones at the base of the arrangement.

Add some shorter flowers until the bunch is full enough and looks fairly even.

Wind some florist's wire firmly around the base of the stalks to hold them all in position. If some of the smaller ones seem loose, then secure them in place with a hot glue gun. Cover the wire with some pretty ribbon tied into a decorative bow.

Finally, to give added depth to the bunch, add some heavier heads, such as peonies, low down near the bow. It is much easier to glue these on with a hot glue gun than to try wiring them.

Using medium to fine gauge florist's wire, attach lengths of wire to several cones and spices, such as star anise, cinnamon or tiny alder cones and beech masts.

Starting with a larger item, such as a single helichrysum flower, make a posy shape around this central feature. Wrap the stems together with florist's tape.

Keep adding to the posy, firmly wrapping the stem of each new ingredient with tape. Tie a ribbon bow at the base of the posy.

Place the posy in a small posy holder and cover the stems with ribbon in the same colour as the bow.

Cut out a double-layered square of net, fill with pot pourri and tie up with ribbon.

Attach the net bag to a small straw hat, using a hot glue gun.

Attach a satin or other ribbon bow with streamers to the hat. The length of the streamers is up to you.

Glue on some dried sea lavender all around the hat as a base for other dried flowers. Continue to add other flowers; use whatever you have available but remember the flowers need to be small.

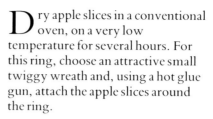

Make a small bundle of lavender by wiring a few fresh or dried stems together, and attach a narrow satin ribbon bow.

Dry apple slices in a conventional oven, on a very low temperature for several hours. For this ring, choose an attractive small twiggy wreath and, using a hot glue gun, attach the apple slices around the ring.

Using a hot glue gun, attach the lavender bundle and bow to a photograph frame.

Add some whole or broken cinnamon sticks, securing them with the hot glue gun. If you want to increase the cinnamon scent, drop some essential cinnamon oil onto the apple slices.

As a finishing touch, add some dried pink rosebuds, using the hot glue gun.

As a final touch, make a decorative ribbon bow in the colour you want and attach it to the ring.

Take a cleaned and varnished old horseshoe. Using narrow satin ribbon, make a long loop and push one end through the top hole on one side of the horseshoe and tie in a knot. Leaving a long length of ribbon, tie the other end through the top hole on the other side of the horseshoe and tie securely.

Using a hot glue gun, attach some dried *Statice dumosa* (sea lavender) to the horseshoe, to act as a base for the other flowers.

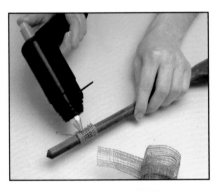

Take a 5 cm (2 in) length of medium gauge florist's wire and bend it in half, into a loop. Glue this loop onto the back of the spoon handle. Wrap a piece of ribbon around the handle to hide the ends of the wire loop and secure with a glue gun.

Add dried roses, helichrysum and larkspur to give a really beautiful finished effect.

Glue on a ribbon bow with short or long streamers, depending on your preference.

Using the glue gun, attach some dried flowers to make a decorative spray above and below the bow.

Choose an attractive box. If it needs recovering this can be done using lining paper and then painting it, or using wrapping paper or wallpaper. Fabric is another possibility, but if you are adding flowers try to keep the fabric as plain as possible. Make wired loops of lace or ribbon and glue them onto the lid of the box with a hot glue gun.

You will need a fabric bow mounted onto a hairslide, some dried flowers and some wired pearls.

Depending on the size of the box, choose fairly large or special flowers rather than a mass of smaller flowers. Flowers dried in silica gel crystals (see page 9) are ideal for this project. The box illustrated is decorated with peonies, which make a wonderful focal point.

Using a hot glue gun, stick on a selection of dried flowers, including sea lavender, either side of the knot in the bow.

Finish the lid with smaller dried flowers to blend with the lace or ribbon and peonies and soften the arrangement.

Finally, make loops of pearls, securing them with wire. Add the loops and some individual pearls to finish the bow.

Collect together a clear or pearlized side comb, some dried and scented rosebuds, some gypsophila, a length of pearls and some reel wire.

Make some loops with the pearl string and the reel wire. Attach these to each end of the comb.

In the centre of the comb, glue on a cluster of the fragrant rosebuds, using a hot glue gun, and add some dainty sprigs of gypsophila.

You will need a large gilt hairslide, 3 dried rose heads, sea lavender, gypsophila and gold cord or ribbon. First attach the sea lavender and 3 roses to the hairslide, using a hot glue gun.

Make some tiny loops with the ribbon and glue those deep into the design.

Finish the slide by adding dainty sprigs of gypsophila to lighten the overall effect.

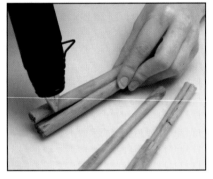

Take 5 cinnamon sticks and glue them together in a bundle, using a hot glue gun.

Wrap a ribbon around the bundle of cinnamon sticks and tie in a decorative bow.

Use whole bay leaves, which can either be gathered from a bush in your own garden, or that of a neighbour, or bought in a jar intended for culinary purposes. Paint over both sides of the leaves with gold paint.

To create different finishes, use several different golds or a bronze or copper colour. Allow the leaves to dry on an old cake cooling rack.

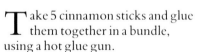

Glue on some dried sea lavender, with the flowers flowing along the bundle rather than across it. Add any other dried flowers you wish. If you want to increase the cinnamon scent, drop a little cinnamon essential oil onto the decoration.

Having wrapped up your parcel, attach the gilded leaves with a hot glue gun and add some nuts or dried flowers.

You will need some slices of dried apple, some wire and a selection of small dried flowers, beech masts and some ribbon. Glue the apple slices together to make a circle.

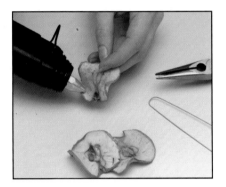

Drill 2 small holes through the top of each walnut and thread through a length of gold cord.

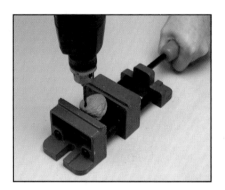

Thread some florist's wire through the top of your circle to make a hanging loop. Twist the wire firmly to secure it.

Using a hot glue gun, add some small alder cones in a group on the top of each walnut.

Decorate with the flowers or beech masts and glue on a couple of ribbon bows, in this case one in green and one in gold.

Finish the decoration with small sprigs of dried sea lavender. To scent the decoration, sprinkle a couple of drops of pot pourri essential oil onto the cones.

Take a pre-formed sphere of dried flower foam. Make a long loop with some ribbon and twist a reasonably long length of wire around the base of the loop, leaving a 'leg' to go through the ball. Pass the wire through the ball until the base of the loop is embedded in the foam. Trim the wire to within 1 cm (½ in) and bend it back into the foam.

Assemble some gilded nigella heads, grasses, dried sea lavender and beech masts or cones. You will also need some gold ribbon or cord. Either make a plain cracker of your own or use a sparsely decorated bought one.

Using a hot glue gun, glue a selection of nuts onto the foam, being fairly liberal with the glue.

Using a hot glue gun, attach the ingredients to one side of the cracker.

Once the ball is completely covered with nuts, check for glimpses of the grey foam and, if there are any, cover them with some dried nigella seed heads. Spray the ball well with a polyurethane matt or satin varnish.

Once you are happy with the design, add some tiny loops of gold ribbon or cord, making sure that the base of each loop is well hidden.

SILK FLOWER DESIGNS

W hen creating a table centre arrangement, it is important not to make it too tall as this can obstruct people's view of those opposite and tends to dominate the table. Choose a fairly low basket and fill with dried flower foam or use a piece of cork as a base and place the foam on top. Cover the foam with moss to make sure it is completely hidden.

A silk posy makes a pretty gift for someone who is unwell. Posy holders can be purchased from florists and craft shops and make the task of making posies far easier. Begin by covering the foam in the posy holder with a selection of silk leaves to form the base of the posy. This not only covers the green foam base but also helps to pad out the display.

Place the silk leaves you are using in position first. They should make an oval shape if the arrangement is intended for a rectangular or oval table, or a circle if it is meant for a square or circular table. In this arrangement small artificial pears have been used to give an added interesting feature.

Add the flowers, starting with smaller blooms and then adding the larger items. In this case, the roses are the main features of the posy. A variety of shapes and forms adds to the interest of the bouquet.

Lastly, add the flowers. When using silk flowers there is a vast and unlimited choice of flowers from all seasons and all climates but it makes an arrangement more realistic if you can use flowers from just one season. Spring and autumn flowers mixed together will immediately give away the secret that you have used silk flowers.

Make sure that the back of the posy looks neat and professionally finished. If necessary, add some extra leaves to cover any untidy stalks, then decorate the stem of the posy holder with ribbons tied into bows.

C ollect together silk flowers and leaves of your choice and a plain greetings card – these can be bought from many craft shops and outlets.

Start by gluing the leaves in a curved design or a 'C' shape on the face of the card. This creates the basic shape of the floral display.

A basket decorated with silk flowers makes a particularly pretty container for pot pourri or any small gift. Choose your flowers and ribbons to co-ordinate with both the pot pourri going inside the basket as well as the room that the basket is going to be in. Firmly attach the flowers to the edge of the basket, starting wherever you wish.

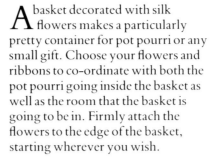

Trim away as much stalk as possible from the flowers so the card is not too bulky, then glue the flowers in position. Pearls or ribbons can be added in small loops to decorate the design, if wished.

Make sure the rim of the basket is well covered with flowers so the design is not too sparse. The best glue to use is that from a hot glue gun as any other craft glue takes too long to set and involves a great deal of time spent holding the flowers in position.

When the rim is completely covered, make some ribbon loops in the colour of your choice – these can look very attractive and add a colour that was unavailable in the flowers you used. Attach them to the basket with glue.

A ny basket would be suitable for this project but the lighter and daintier it is the better; sweet peas are not large overpowering flowers and a heavy rustic basket might not work quite as well. Start by one handle and glue on the silk flowers and leaves, making them look as natural as possible.

F ill the chosen flat-backed basket with some dried flower foam, using a hot glue gun to secure it in position.

A hot glue gun is essential as speed is of the essence when attaching the flowers to the handle. Continue adding flowers, making them look as though they were growing up the handle. In this case the tendrils add a really natural and realistic touch. Glue bows on either side of the handle.

Cover the foam with moss. Reindeer moss is easily available from craft shops and gives a good covering without preventing the stems going through it.

As this is such an open weave basket a lining is useful, and in this case a Nottingham lace handkerchief is placed in the basket together with bubble bath pearls and some dried rosebuds.

Arrange the silk flowers of your choice in the basket, starting with larger blooms and adding smaller ones for padding as you go along. Make sure the basket is attractive from all angles, particularly from below, as you will probably be looking up at the arrangement when it is on the wall.

You will need a couple of sprays of silk sweet pea flowers with some foliage and tendrils, a plastic hairband and some ribbon.

You will need 1 or 2 side combs, some silk spray carnations and some leaves, gold cord, wired pearls and some reel wire.

Separate the sweet pea flowers and leaves from their stalks or sprays. Individually attach each leaf and flower to the hairband, using a hot glue gun.

Using a hot glue gun, first attach the leaves to the comb(s) and then the silk carnations.

Ensure you add some tendrils as they make a huge difference to the finished design. Add a ribbon bow at each end of the hairband in a toning colour.

Make small wired loops with the gold cord or ribbon and glue these on to the comb(s), then as a finishing touch add some small wired pearls.

Y ou will need 2 tortoiseshell hair combs and some silk orchids with leaves.

Separate the blooms and leaves from the orchid spray, then attach some leaves to one of the combs, using a hot glue gun.

Glue a couple of flowers onto the comb. Repeat the operation with the second comb to make a matching pair.

Y ou will need some silk rosebuds and some tortoiseshell hairslides.

Separate the rosebuds and leaves. Using a hot glue gun attach the leaves to the hairslides in an attractive pattern.

Add the rosebuds; you can use all the same colour or alternate between 2 different colours.

PRESSED FLOWER DESIGNS

Arrange a small design on the outside flap of the envelopes and also on one corner of the sheets of notepaper. You may like to leave some sheets blank for continuation sheets.

Glue the pressed flowers and leaves firmly in place with latex adhesive, applying it with a needle or piece of florist's wire, and then cover with a piece of clear film.

Leave the paper and envelopes in a large box with some highly scented pot pourri for a few weeks, then tie the sheets of paper with a toning ribbon and place in their presentation box.

Use a piece of firm card and arrange pressed leaves in an oval, leaving spaces for flowers to be added.

Tuck in a selection of flowers and dainty fillers – in this case, alchemilla and roses – then glue firmly with latex adhesive, applying it with a needle or piece of florist's wire.

Place in any frame of your choice, making sure the glass is clean and that the back of the picture is well sealed.

U se a pre-cut photograph mount – or use the template on page 93 – and arrange some pressed leaves around the opening.

Add some more pressed flowers and other pieces to fill out the design.

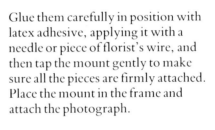

U sing either a piece of card folded to size or a ready-made blank greetings card, arrange a pretty design on it with pressed flowers and leaves.

Glue them carefully in position with latex adhesive, applying it with a needle or piece of florist's wire, and then tap the mount gently to make sure all the pieces are firmly attached. Place the mount in the frame and attach the photograph.

Glue the arrangement firmly with latex adhesive, applying it with a needle or piece of florist's wire, and then cover carefully with a piece of clear film.

Place the card and its envelope in a box with highly scented rose petals, or some rose-scented pot pourri, and leave it for a few weeks until the card has taken up the rose fragrance.

Use a plain piece of card or a specially made blank greetings card. In this case the card has a silver edge. Arrange some pressed leaves on the card to begin the design.

Add some pressed fern and some red roses or other flowers of your choice. Finish the design with a dainty filler such as gypsophila.

Glue the flowers and leaves carefully with some latex adhesive, applying it with a needle or piece of florist's wire, and then cover the design with a piece of clear film.

Use a plain notebook, with a cover that is either a dark colour or very pale, such as cream or white. Arrange some pressed leaves on the front to start the design.

Add some pressed flowers, using fairly bright colours if they are against a dark background, to make a strong contrast.

Carefully stick down the flowers and leaves with latex adhesive, applying it with a needle or piece of florist's wire, and then cover with a piece of clear film.

B lack forms a chic backdrop for many pale plants. Here, the pale blue and eau-de-nil colours sit very prettily. Begin by coating the lid of a small black box with special 'two pack' gloss varnish. Place sprays of mugwort leaves, underside uppermost, in the left hand corners.

Add two mugwort sprays to the right hand corners. Now, carefully splitting a leaf spray, create a fan shape in the top centre of the lid.

Just below the fan, in the centre of the box, form a small cluster of mugwort leaves and, on top, fix a little arrangement of blue lobelia and cornflower florets. Seal the design with two thin coats of varnish.

T ake a blank piece of card and, using tweezers, arrange some dried leaves on it (in this case maidenhair fern), then add some dried pink larkspur and some grasses.

Carefully stick down all the leaves and flowers with some latex adhesive, applying it with a needle or piece of florist's wire, then cover the design with a piece of clear film.

To scent the bookmark, place it with some pot pourri in a box and cover. Leave for a few weeks to take up the smell of the pot pourri.

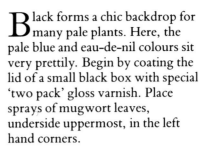

The design templates on the following pages are printed on 1-cm (⅜-in) grids to help you copy them more easily. To reproduce the design, draw up a grid making the squares the same, double or three times the size they are here, according to the size you wish your project to be. Copy the design, one square at a time, on to your grid. When completed, you can cut it out and use it like an ordinary paper pattern.

SCENTED TEA COSY
(pages 26-7)

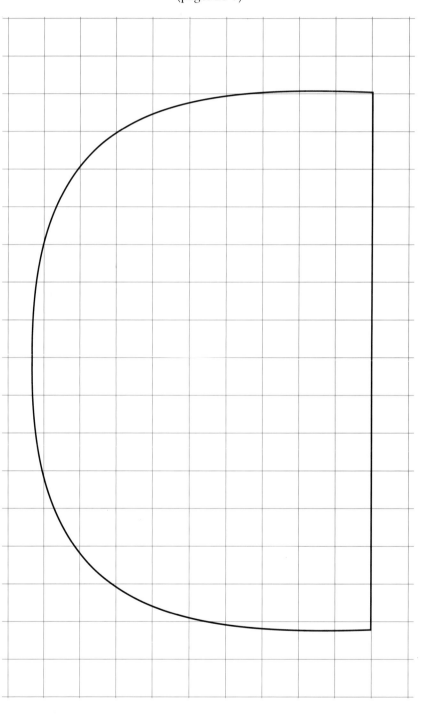

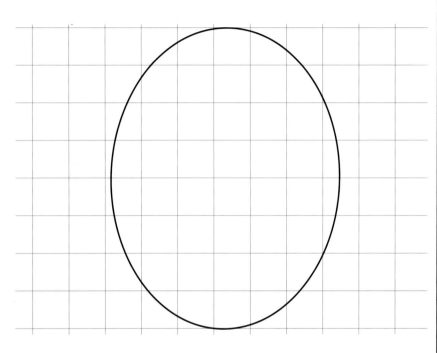

LAVENDER AND HERB SACHET
(pages 16-17)

CHRISTMAS STOCKING
(page 72)

HERBAL HOT MAT
(pages 28-9)

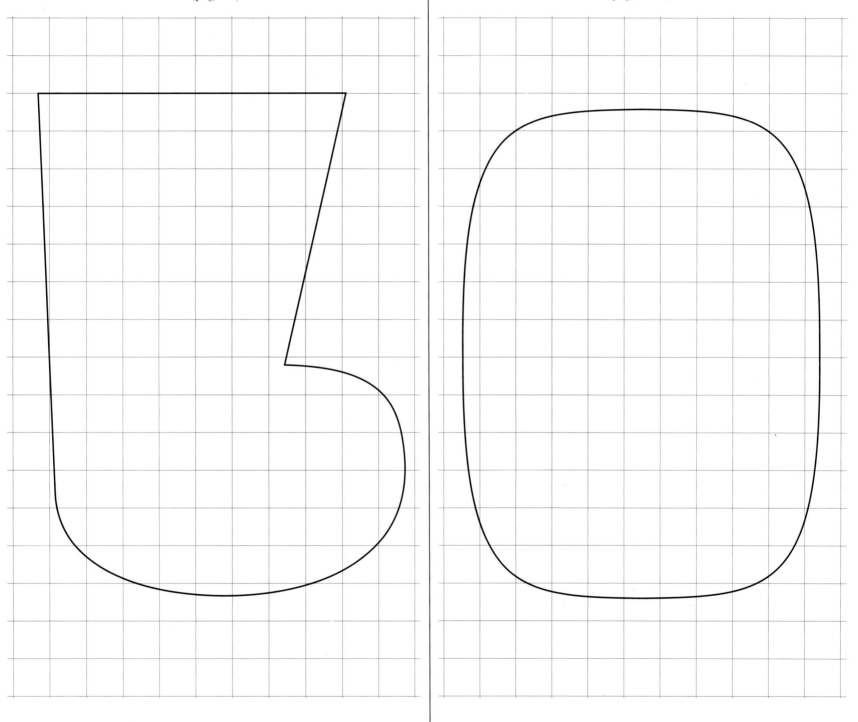

GLOSSARY

Below are listed some of the essential oils available from herbalists, with a brief description of their scent and their properties. A good herbalist will have further information on the uses of these and other essential oils.

BASIL A sweet and spicy scented oil, basil has a calming, uplifting effect and helps alleviate fatigue and insomnia.

BENZOIN Benzoin is an antiseptic oil with a relaxing and warming effect. It helps rid the skin of impurities.

BERGAMOT With a sweet and fruity scent and refreshing properties, bergamot oil is excellent in a bath, as a massage oil, or in pot pourris and sweet powders.

BLACK PEPPER With a woody and spicy scent, black pepper oil has stimulating and warming properties, and is particularly useful for relieving muscular aches.

CARDAMOM Cardamom oil has a warm and spicy aroma, and is often used in India in perfumes and incenses. The oil is refreshing and invigorating, and useful in baths or bath products.

CARROT SEED This sweet and earthy scented oil is helpful for dry skin conditions and it is thought to help restore the skin's elasticity.

CEDARWOOD A balsamic-woody scented oil, cedarwood oil has calming properties, and it is useful for oily skin and hair, and as an antiseptic and insect-repellent.

CHAMOMILE A deep blue-coloured oil, with calming and soothing properties, chamomile is particularly useful for insomnia and skin irritations.

CINNAMON With a warm, sweet and spicy scent, cinnamon oil is known for its invigorating properties. It must be heavily diluted before using.

CLARY SAGE A spicy and floral scented oil, clary sage oil soothes and relaxes.

CLOVE Clove oil has a woody and spicy scent and stimulating properties.

CYPRESS Cypress oil has a sweet pine scent and astringent properties, and helps varicose veins and broken capillaries.

EUCALYPTUS An oil with a strong medicinal scent, eucalyptus oil is useful for relieving cold symptoms and sinus conditions. It is stimulating, an antiseptic, and an insect repellent.

EUCALYPTUS CITRIADORA With a fresh lemony scent, eucalyptus citriadora oil has refreshing and astringent properties.

FENNEL Fennel oil has a sweet fresh scent with aniseed undertones.

GERANIUM An oil with a highly floral and green aroma, geranium oil is useful for treating anxiety and dry skin. It is particularly useful in baths, massage oils and skin creams, and as an insect repellent and refreshing astringent.

GINGER With a warm, fresh and spicy scent, this oil is popular in perfume blends. It is a stimulating oil, suitable for baths and bath products.

GRAPEFRUIT Grapefruit oil is citrus-scented and has astringent properties.

JASMINE With a highly floral and exotic scent, this oil is perfect for perfumes. It also helps dry skin conditions.

JUNIPER Juniper oil helps oily skin and is excellent for a freshing bath to stimulate circulation.

LAVENDER Sweet smelling and antiseptic, lavender oil is useful for

inflamations of the skin, burns, wounds and bites, as well as in a massage oil or bath. Lavender is also helpful for treating insomnia.

LEMON With its sweet lemon scent, lemon oil is often used in perfumes for its fruity note. It is also an antiseptic and astringent for the skin, and helpful for insect bites.

LEMONGRASS An oil with a grassy lemon scent, lemongrass oil helps problem skins and is useful as an insect repellent.

LIME With a sharp lime scent, lime oil is an astringent, useful for oily skin.

MARJORAM An oil with a sweet herbal scent, marjoram has relaxing properties and is useful to relieve stress, anxiety and insomnia.

MELISSA (LEMON BALM) A sweet-scented oil, melissa oil is calming and uplifting, and useful to ease tension and stress headaches.

NEROLI With a highly floral scent, neroli oil is used in eau de cologne. It has relaxing properties, and is useful to ease anxiety and insomnia, as well as to soothe dry skin.

ORANGE Orange oil is a fruity smelling oil with a refreshing effect.

PATCHOULI With a dry, woody smell, patchouli is used as a fixative in perfumes. As an astringent oil it helps treat problem skin and oily scalps. The oil is also excellent for dry skins and is said to have cell-regenerating properties.

PEPPERMINT Peppermint oil is minty-scented and has a cooling and refreshing effect on the skin.

PETIGRAINE With its sweet floral smell, similar to neroli, petigraine oil is excellent for refreshing massage blends or bath oils.

ROSE A sweet floral-scented oil, rose oil is traditionally used for perfumes. It has a relaxing effect and benefits dry, sensitive skins.

ROSE GERANIUM Often used as a substitute for the similar but more expensive rose oil.

ROSEMARY With a herbaceous scent and stimulating properties, rosemary oil helps the hair and scalp.

SAGE An herbaceous-scented oil, sage oil is useful in baths or in massage oils to relieve aches and pains.

SANDALWOOD With its balsamic, woody scent, sandalwood oil makes an excellent massage oil for men and helps dry, itchy skin.

THYME Thyme oil is a stimulating oil useful in baths to ease aches and pains and to invigorate.

YLANG YLANG With an exotic floral scent, ylang ylang is used in perfumes. It also has a relaxing sedative effect.

INDEX